*IF you want to do something GOOD for a child,
give him an ENVIRONMENT
where he can TOUCH things
as much as he wants.*

Buckminster Fuller

Acknowledgments

As with any creative project there are many folks to thank – kudos to Nili Miller for gathering new ideas, typing them up and trying them out wherever counter space allowed, Zoe Somebody and the creative artistic folks at [i] motion design, Diana and Sue who got the ball rolling and have passed their "baby" onto us... I hope we do you proud! And, as always, to Tom for his never ending supply of patience with my never ending ability to miss every single deadline.

My love to you all.

Published by Ooey Gooey, Inc.

1115 E. Main St.
Box 48
Rochester, NY 14609
800-477-7977

www.ooeygooey.com

ISBN 978-1-60554-377-2

Cover and inside text design and layout by [i] motion design
www.imotiondesign.net

FSC
www.fsc.org

MIX
Paper | Supporting
responsible forestry
FSC® C008955

Even More Fizzle, Bubble, Pop & WOW!

Simple Science Experiments for Young Children

Revised Edition by
Lisa Murphy

Redleaf Press®
www.redleafpress.org
800-423-8309

Contents

The Beginning Stuff

Introduction from the Original Edition

This book is a collection of science experiments that will excite any young learner. It has been developed at the urging of teachers who wanted easy reference to successful science activities. The result is a practical resource that can be effectively utilized with children ages three through twelve. All of these experiments have been tried a number of times. They have been adult tested, kid tested, and will work successfully for you. If sometimes you do not arrive at the expected outcome, try again. This approach is part of being a scientist. The experiments are not our own creation. They have existed for many years and have been drawn from various sources. Primarily, they are ideas that have been shared by other early childhood teachers. When we began our program, our goal was to excite the children in our preschool about the notion of "science." Initially, having an educational background in Liberal Art as do many of our colleagues we felt unqualified to teach science to anyone. When we looked at the children, however, our feelings of inadequacies were soon dispelled. We understood that having a positive attitude about science was far more important than having extensive knowledge. Young children don't require detailed explanations of scientific principles. They need the same opportunity we offer in all other areas of learning: the chance to experience it first hand. Simply put, they need to "do" science.

With that in mind, we set out to develop a program in which the children could be active participants. Through our research and practical experimentation we discovered, much to our delight, that anyone can create an exciting and successful science component. Simple materials and basic ingredients of water, air, candles, vinegar, baking soda, salt, eggs, and balloons are readily available at low cost. As you look through our book, you will see that some of the activities are those that the adults demonstrate; but most are those in which the children take part. Through their involvement they learn basic concepts about gravity, air, fire, and water. But at this early level many of the activities simply appear to be like magic to them. Mostly what we want our children to learn is that science is fun. The philosopher Le Rochefoucauld said, "People rarely succeed at anything unless they have fun doing it." We wish you fun and success in developing or expanding your science program for young children.

Diana, Sue and Donna
1992

A Story for You from Lisa

Back in 1997 when I began doing my workshops I kept running into two women who were doing this fantastic science workshop that participants simply referred to as "Fizzle Bubble". I checked it out – they had experiments that fizzled, bubbled and popped and many activities that made you say WOW!

I bought their book. I used their book. I inadvertently stained the book with vinegar, grape juice, food coloring and baking soda. Many pages were dog-eared for ease of reference and others were simply falling out! The book was disintegrating from overuse – I had to get another copy! And while I'm at it, I'll get one for my mom, my director, my friend who needs some new ideas... you get the picture!

The experiments that they were teaching us in the workshop were EASY! They were SIMPLE! And they were done with supplies and materials I already had in the classroom and in my kitchen! I really was able to bolster up my science program. I realized I did not need to have a degree in science to be successful. Further readings and deeper explorations assisted me in realizing that EVERYTHING around us was science – not just the activity we pulled out at 10:15 AM on Friday morning.

After seeing them at workshops I started talking with the ladies – the "Fizzle Bubble Ladies" as they were called! I learned their real names were Diana and Sue. We ran into each other more and more as I began doing more workshops. We became friends, making sure we met up with each other at a conference, even if it was just for a quick "hello!" before our individual sessions.

I don't really remember when the topic came up, but there was a point when I shared with them about my early years growing up in Livermore, California and the amazing nursery school I was able to go to. It was then that Diana shared with me that not only did she grow up in the house across the street from Mary's Nursery School – but that her mother used to teach there!

This connection to such an important part of my past was small yet very significant. We started to make more of an effort to stay connected. We began sharing ideas with each other, chatting after workshop sessions and staying in touch between conferences.

Diana became my long distance "mom", always checking in with me, making sure I was staying healthy, not burning the candle at both ends, not traveling too much, picking me up from the airport when I was in her area, supporting me in my expanding efforts to take OOEY GOOEY, INC. nationwide.

Then in 1999 while wrapping up an afternoon breakout session at a conference at California State University, Hayward, Diana came running into the workshop room asking, "So – how did you like your surprise?"

"Surprise?" I asked, "What surprise?"

"You didn't know?"

"Know WHAT??!!"

She pointed to two ladies in the audience, "Surprise!"

I looked in the direction she was indicating – there were two ladies, sitting together, eyes bright, smiles beaming... It was Miss Mary and Miss Nancy! My teachers from nursery school! I had not seen them since I was about ten. What an emotional reunion that was! Thank goodness my friend and colleague Shalimar Moniz was there to wrap up the workshop for me as I melted into tears of surprise and happiness!

I will be forever grateful to Diana for coordinating that reunion between me and my teachers.

It was in 2002 that our relationship took on a "business" angle. After 15 years of doing the Fizzle Bubble workshops, Diana and Sue were looking to retire from doing the sessions but still wanted to make sure that the information was getting out to the schools, teachers and providers. We spent about a year talking, negotiating, planning and discussing the best way that could happen. In 2003 Diana and Sue asked if we would officially be interested in acquiring the copyright to their book and workshop. We agreed.

So here we are.

We have changed the look and added new activities, yet the goal is still the same – making sure the information is getting to the folks who need it! Science happens every day! It is not just what we "do" when the lesson plan calls for it.

Watching rollie pollies meander through the grass is science, splashing in the puddles is science, watching the heaps of snow melt and the flowers nudge up through the dirt is science. Living, breathing, eating, growing... it is all science. Our goal is to assist you in seeing that science is happening all around every day. Please use the book to plan activities but remember that science is not limited to the activities!

It is assumed that adults and/or older children are providing supervision and are acting as facilitators while the children complete the steps involved in the experiment! Although a few of the activities might be what you'd call "watch the teacher" activities, the majority of them are designed for the children to do themselves!!!!

...given a rich environment – with open ended raw materials – children can be encouraged and trusted to take a large part in the design of their own learning. (Science with Young Children, Bess-Gene Holt, 1989, pg. 18)

So head on out there – sift through the cupboards, dig through the shed, start saving plastic bottles and collecting corks. Save the rubber bands from the newspaper and those annoying internet CDs you get in the mail every day. Clean off the shelf that is piled with dusty stuff you never use and make a fresh new Fizzle Bubble shelf for you and the children!

I think you will be glad that you did!

All my best,

Lisa Murphy

Phone: (800) 477-7977
Email: LTAC@ooeygooey.com
Web: www.ooeygooey.com

Your Fizzle Bubble Shopping List

We have compiled a list for you of everything you will need in order to do the experiments in this book. We have divided the list into FIXED EQUIPMENT and CONSUMABLES. Meaning – materials you always have around and ingredients you need to replenish as they run out. Enjoy!

FIXED EQUIPMENT

3" x 5" index cards
Baby food jars
Baking pan
Balls (golf, ping pong)
Berry baskets
Bottles and jars of various assorted
    sizes and shapes
Bowls of assorted sizes
Broom
Can opener
Cardboard
CD's
Cheesecloth
Chicken bones
Clothes pins
Coat hangers (metal)
Corks
Cotton string
Cups
Eyedroppers

Film canisters
Fly swatters
Funnels
Handkerchief
Hot glue gun
Ice cream containers
    (plastic and paper ones)
Magazines
Marbles
Measuring cups
Measuring spoons
Metal spoons
Old hose
Paint brushes
Paper clips
Pennies
Permanent markers
Pie tins
Pipettes
Pitchers

Plastic eggs
Plastic party cups
    (those clear ones)
Plastic tubing
Potato peeler
Push pins
PVC pipe
Recycled dish soap bottles
    (and tops from them)
Rubber bands
Safety pins
Scissors
Sensory tub
Sponges
T-shirt (white)
Tuning forks
Water
Wine glasses
Wooden spoons
Yogurt containers

CONSUMABLES

Alka-Seltzer®
Baking soda
Balloons
Blueberry syrup
Borax
Cabbage
Carrots
Celery
Club soda, 7-Up® or some other
    clear carbonated beverage
Coffee filters
Cooking oil
Cornstarch
Corn syrup
Curling ribbon
Dish soap
Dried peas
Eggs
Evaporated milk
Food coloring

Glue
Grape juice
Heavy cream
Honey
Ice
Jell-O®
Kleenex®
Lifesavers®
Liquid starch
Liquid watercolors
Markers
Matches
Mineral oil
Newspaper
Oil
Paper
Paper towels
Paper towel rolls
Paprika
Pasta

Pepper
Raisins
Rice
Rubbing alcohol
Salt
Saran Wrap®
Shampoo
Shortening
Straws
Sugar
Tape (masking, scotch, packing)
Toilet paper rolls
Toothpicks
Vinegar
Votive candles
Wax paper
Whipping cream
Yeast
Ziploc® bags

The Experiments

Air Is Everywhere

Materials

- A large bowl or tub
- A cup
- Water

Process

1. Fill the bowl with water about ¾ of the way up.
2. Hold the cup upside down and push it to the bottom of the bowl.
3. Tip the cup slightly and watch what happens!

Explanation

Although we can't see the air, it is all around us! The cup was filled with air when it was pushed into the water and as it was tipped, the air escaped in the form of bubbles.

Balloon Blowup

Materials

- Recycled water bottle
- 9 inch balloon
- 2 tsp baking soda
- ½ cup vinegar
- Funnel

Process

1. Use the funnel to put the baking soda into the balloon.
2. Pour the vinegar into the bottle.
3. Place the mouth of balloon over the bottle opening.
4. Lift the balloon, letting the baking soda fall into the bottle.
5. Watch what happens inside the bottle and to the balloon.

Explanation

Soda and vinegar react to form carbon dioxide. Carbon dioxide inflates the balloon.

Balloon Vibrations

Materials

- Large (9-12 inch) balloons

Note !

Have one balloon for each child.

Process

1. Blow up a large size balloon for each child and tie it with a knot.
2. With a hand on each side, hold the balloon.
3. Talk into the balloon and feel the vibration of your words.

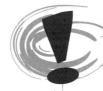

Explanation

Sound is made by vibrations. The sounds from the children talking will vibrate the balloon.

Bendable Bones

Materials

- Small chicken bones (such as the wish bone or bones from the chicken wing with meat thoroughly removed)
- Large glass jar
- Vinegar

Process

1. Place a bone in a jar.
2. Pour vinegar into the jar until the bone is completely covered.
3. Let contents sit for five to seven days.
4. Remove the bone from the jar
5. Now bend the bone!

Explanation

It is the calcium in the bone that makes it strong and hard. When the vinegar dissolves the calcium, the remaining substance is flexible.

Best Bubble Solution

Materials

- 6 cups water
- 2 cups Dawn® dish soap
- Sensory/large tub
- Various bubble tools such as: straws, paper towel rolls, flyswatters, berry baskets, your hands, 6 pack rings, PVC pipes with cheesecloth on one end, etc...

Note !

Dawn® is one of the few dish soaps that contain glycerin. Glycerin assists in making stronger, longer lasting bubbles.

Hint

Wash bubble tools with vinegar and water to remove the sticky bubble residue.

Process

1. Combine the water and the dish soap in a large tub.
2. Allow the children to blow bubbles with an assortment of bubble tools.
3. Ask the children what other things might work as bubble blowers, and then test those out as well.

Explanation

Bubbles are the perfect example of surface tension! Surface tension casues the surface of a liquid to pull together and create a "skin" on the surface of the liquid. Bubbles are actually thin balls of liquid with air trapped in the center.

Better Butter

Materials

- 3-4 Small containers or jars with tight fitting lids
- Whipping cream

Process

1. Fill the jars 1/3 of the way full with whipping cream.
2. Fasten the lids tightly.
3. Shake the jars! NOTE: This process takes about 10-15 minutes! Be patient and take turns shaking!
4. Have children observe the changes as the cream turns into butter!

Hint

Have crackers available so the children can taste the finished product!

Explanation

The whipping cream is coagulated by agitation and turns into butter.

Variation

Add 1 teaspoon sour cream to the jar. This ingredient will decrease the amount of time it takes to make the butter.

Add a clean marble to one or two of the jars to see if that changes the time it takes to make the butter!

The Big Fizz

Materials

- Large soda pop bottle
- Cooking oil
- Liquid watercolor
- Alka-Seltzer® tablets
- Water

Process

1. Fill the bottle ¾ full with oil.
2. Fill the rest of the bottle with colored water. The darker the better.
3. Drop an Alka-Seltzer® tablet into the bottle and watch!

Explanation

Oil is lighter (less dense) than water so it rises to the top of the bottle when the water is added. Alka-Seltzer® tablets produce carbon dioxide gas bubbles. These bubbles carry the colored water to the top of the bottle. When the bubbles pop the water sinks back down to the bottom of the bottle.

The Blob

Materials

- 1 cup white glue
- 1 cup liquid starch
- Food coloring or liquid watercolor
- Bowl
- Ziploc® bags

Process

1. Mix the glue and the color in a bowl.
2. Slowly pour the liquid starch into the glue, stirring constantly with your hands.
3. Keep stirring until the mixture holds together.
4. Use your imagination and let the children play with the blob. When they are finished it can be kept in Ziploc® baggies.

Explanation

Similar to Flubber (pg 47), this is another one of those wonderful non-Newtonian fluids, which acts as both a solid and a liquid at the same time!

Bubbling Eruption

Materials

- ½ cup dishwashing liquid
- ¾ cup vinegar
- 1 cup water
- 4 - 5 drops red food color or liquid watercolor
- 1 recycled 2 liter soda bottle
- ½ cup baking soda
- Funnel
- Small pitcher
- The sandbox

Process

1. Mix soap, vinegar, water, and food coloring in the pitcher.
2. Push the 2 liter bottle into the sand.
3. Put the baking soda into the 2 liter bottle.
4. Now pour the liquid mixture (from the pitcher) into the 2 liter bottle!

Variation

Try it again with only vinegar – use 2 cups of it – with no water or soap added. How is the eruption different?

Explanation

Mixing baking soda and vinegar creates carbon dioxide gas. The gas pushes the colored mixture up simulating a bubbling eruption! Dishwashing liquid extends the reaction time and thickens the lava.

Cabbage Clues

Materials

- 1 large purple cabbage
- Measuring cups and spoons
- Clear plastic party cups (one for each child)
- Vinegar (have a 1 gallon container on hand – you might not need it all – but you want to be prepared!)
- Baking soda (have a large box ready to go!)

Variation

Try adding any of these to the cabbage juice to see the results: orange juice, milk of magnesia, lemon juice or cream of tartar.

Explanation

The cabbage juice serves as an indicator. By adding a variety of substances to it you can determine which substance is an acid and which substance is a base. When cabbage juice is used as an indicator acids will turn the juice pink and a base will turn it greenish-blue.

Process

Day One

1. After taking a look at the purple cabbage together, boil the cabbage until it is completely white.
2. Strain the cabbage but reserve the purple colored water.
3. Allow the purple water to cool overnight in the fridge.
4. Save the cabbage – either for a snack (some do like it) or to remember the process of how the purple liquid was obtained. You will want to eventually discard this cabbage, but be sure to store it in the fridge until you do.

Day Two

1. Give each child a clear cup.
2. Fill 1/3 of the clear cups with purple cabbage juice.
3. Add about 2 TBS of vinegar to the cabbage water and notice how the color changes from purple to pink.
4. Now add a few pinches of baking soda to the cup, one pinch at a time, and watch as the liquid changes back from pink to purple!
5. Repeat the process of adding vinegar and then baking soda to create the color changes until the children are finished exploring!

Clear Blue Sea

Materials

- Recycled water bottle with the label removed
- Distilled water
- Mineral oil
- Blue food color or liquid watercolor
- Hot glue gun (to secure the lid)

Process

1. Fill the bottle 2/3 full with blue colored water.
2. Fill the rest of the bottle with mineral oil. Be sure to fill to the very top. Do not leave any air space. I suggest you hot glue the lid back on in order to keep it securely closed!
3. Gently rock and shake the bottle back and forth and sideways to see the waves.

Explanation

Oil and water do not mix. When you rock the bottle, the oil and water move against each other but do not mix together.

Coat Hanger Chime

Materials

- Some metal coat hangers
- Long pieces of cotton string

Process

1. Tie the cotton string to the hook part of a coat hanger.
2. Help the children wrap the other end of the string around one of their fingers a couple of times.
3. Ask the children to place their fingers near their ears and have them gently bang the hanger on a table or the floor.

Explanation

The coat hanger vibrates when it strikes another hard object and makes a noise. Vibrations travel better through cotton string than through the air so the sound is amplified when it's held near their ears.

Coffee Filter Science

Materials

- Coffee filters
- Assorted brands of black markers
- Clear cup or baby food jar for every child
- Water

Hint

"Smelly markers" work the best!

Variation

Compare and contrast the results of various brands of markers. What happens when you use a permanent marker?

Process

1. Make a big black dot in the middle of the coffee filter.
2. Fold the coffee filter in half (once), then again (twice), and now a third time to create a triangle.
3. Fill the clear cups with a small amount of water – just enough to cover the tip of the coffee filter triangle.
4. Place the marker coated tip of the coffee filter in the water and see what happens!

Explanation

Coffee filters are very absorbent. A small amount of water can travel very rapidly through a coffee filter. Black markers are made up of different colored pigments and water. When the filter began soaking up water, it carried the pigments from the ink up with it. Eventually the colors in the ink separate out and will become visible.

Cold Water Insulation

Materials

- Bowl of ice water
- Shortening

Process

1. Have each child place both their index fingers in the bowl of ice water. How does it feel?
2. Remove your fingers and cover ONE index finger with a generous coat of shortening.
3. Place BOTH fingers back into the ice water. Now how does it feel?

Explanation

Fat provides insulation. The finger with the shortening on it will not feel cold.

Colored Carrot

Materials

- A carrot (1 for each child)
- Tall plastic cups
- Water
- Liquid watercolor (red works best) or food coloring

Process

1. Cut the tip off each carrot.
2. Fill the cups ½ full with colored water.
3. Place the carrots in the cups and let them sit for several days.
4. Cut each carrot in half and let the children examine the inside.

Hint

When exploring the colored carrots be sure to provide an unused carrot in order to compare the two!

Explanation

The water was absorbed from the bottom of the carrot and carried through its entire structure. This is the same way that plants and trees gather water with their roots to grow.

Colored Celery

Materials

- 4 celery stalks with the leaves attached
- 4 clear cups
- Liquid watercolor or food coloring
- 4 paper towels
- Potato peeler
- Water

Explanation

Plants grow by absorbing water through their capillaries. These tiny "straws" suck water up and use it to make food. By observing the different stages of the celery you are actually able to see the capillaries at work.

Process

1. Cut each piece of celery approximately 3-4 inches from the top of the stalk.
2. Fill the 4 cups ½ way up with water. Add some drops of color to each cup (Purple or red work the best).
3. Place a stalk of celery in each of the 4 cups. Set aside.
4. After two hours, remove 1 stalk from the colored water and place it on a paper towel. Write on the towel "2 hours."
5. Use the potato peeler to peel the rounded side of the celery. You will be able to see how far the water has traveled up the stalk.
6. After two more hours have passed repeat step 4, and remove a second piece of celery. Mark this towel "4 hours."
7. Continue this process until all the stalks have been removed. See how long it takes for the leaves to show color.
8. Have the children examine each stage of the experiment.

Cork Lift Off

Materials

- 1 small bottle (10-12 oz.)
- 1 cork that fits tightly into the bottle opening
- ¼ cup vinegar
- 1 tsp baking soda
- 1 thumb tack
- Curling ribbon

Process

1. Pour the vinegar into the bottle.
2. Carefully and quickly, put the baking soda into the bottle.
3. Immediately cork the bottle.
4. Aim the cork away from people and watch the lift off!

Hint

Attach the curling ribbon to the cork with the thumb tack to make visual tracking of the cork easier.

Explanation

Propulsion! Vinegar and baking soda creates carbon dioxide gas. This creates pressure inside the bottle which then sends the cork into the air.

Dancing Noodles

Materials

- Uncooked pasta noodles broken into small pieces
- Glass jar
- ½ cup water
- ¼ cup vinegar
- ½ tsp baking soda

Variation

1. Try a variety of noodles in the same glass! Try rigatoni noodles, alphabet noodles, and salad macaroni all at the same time! Watch the noodles dance at different tempos.

2. Try any of these in this activity and notice the similarities and differences:

(a) *Cooked* spaghetti, cut into small pieces
(b) Straws cut into small pieces
(c) Raisins
(d) Dried peas

3. Instead of using baking soda and vinegar, try using any clear carbonated liquid such as 7-Up® or club soda.

Process

1. Mix the water and vinegar in the glass jar.
2. In the same jar, slowly add the baking soda, pinch by pinch.
3. Drop the pieces of pasta into the jar and watch what happens!

Explanation

The vinegar and baking soda form bubbles which cling to the pasta. The gas bubbles make the pasta lighter and the pasta rises to the top of the glass. When the gas bubbles burst the pasta falls to the bottom. Gas bubbles attach to the pasta again and the cycle is repeated.

Egg in the Glass

Materials

- Drinking glass filled ½ way with water
- An egg
- Pie tin
- Toilet paper roll
- Broom

Note !

This is an experiment that is demonstrated to the children.

Hint

Be sure to try this at home a few times before bringing it in to show the children! Practice makes perfect!

Process

1. Position the glass of water near the edge of a table or counter.
2. Put the pie tin on top of the glass of water. Be sure it is directly over the center of the glass.
3. Stand the toilet paper roll in the center of the pie tin.
4. Place the egg in the top of the toilet paper roll.
5. Take the broom and stand in front of the egg. Step on the bristles of the broom and pull back on the handle. The idea here is that when you release the broom handle, it will hit the edge of the pie tin and the egg will tumble into the glass of water.
6. Let go of the broom handle and watch the egg!

Explanation

This experiment is an example of inertia. The broom handle acts as an external force and it causes both the pie tin and the toilet paper roll to move, but the egg is at rest and therefore it stays at rest, and drops into the glass.

Eggshell Power

Materials

- 4 empty, dried eggshell halves
- Several magazines of varying weights
- Smooth table top

Process

1. Place eggshells on a table with a smooth even surface.
2. Position them with the rounded side up so that each one serves as the corner of an imaginary square on the table.
3. How many magazines can be placed on top of the eggshells before the shells begin to crumble?
4. Count aloud as you place magazines (gently) on top of the eggs until the collapse occurs.

Explanation

Because of their dome shape, eggshells can withstand a surprising amount of pressure!

Egg in the Bottle

Materials

- Hard boiled egg with shell removed
- Quart or half gallon glass bottle with an opening that is smaller than the circumference of the egg
- Matches
- Newspaper
- An extra adult assistant

Note !

This is an experiment that is demonstrated to the children.

Variation

You can use a 9 inch balloon instead of the egg. Fill the balloon with water making it the size of a baseball and then follow the same process.

Process

1. Place the egg on top of the bottle. Notice how the egg will not fit into the bottle. Is there a way to get it in?? YES!
2. Accordion fold a 4 x 4 inch piece of newspaper.
4. Have your adult assistant light the bottom of the newspaper with a match.
5. Now quickly put the burning paper inside the bottle, making sure the flame is burning from the bottom up.
6. Immediately and carefully place the egg on top of the bottle, and watch what happens!

Explanation

The burning paper heats the air inside the bottle, which causes the air to expand. After the flame dies out the air cools. When this happens, the air pressure outside the bottle is greater than the pressure inside the bottle which forces the egg down into the bottle.

Exploding Colors

Materials

- Pie tin
- Evaporated milk (at room temperature)
- Food coloring
- Toothpicks
- Dish soap
- Can opener

Process

1. Pour the evaporated milk into the pie tin so that the bottom is completely covered.
2. Add three or four drops of food color to the milk, one drop at a time. Use different colors and keep the colors separated from each other.
3. Dip the tip of a toothpick into the dish soap.
4. Touch the soap covered toothpick tip into the center of each droplet of coloring.
5. Watch as the colors explode right before your eyes!

Variation

Whole milk can be used instead of evaporated milk.

Explanation

When soap touches the milk, the surface tension is broken and the color droplets are dispersed instantly throughout the liquid.

Exploding Soda

Materials

- Several unopened 2-liter bottles of soda (one diet and one regular)
- Wintergreen Lifesavers® (FYI - Breathsavers® do not work well)
- Thin straw or a coffee stirrer

Note !

This activity is best done outside in the middle of the playground or on the grass. Have enough materials on hand to do this one a few times!

Explanation

Carbon dioxide bubbles need a place to attach themselves. These places are called nucleation sites. The porous surface of the candy provides lots of these nucleation sites! All the carbon dioxide bubbles which were released when you opened the soda need a place to adhere to. As the little gas bubbles rush to the nucleation sites they make even bigger bubbles which then burst out of the top of the soda bottle!

Process

1. Carefully open the bottle of regular soda. Position the bottle on the ground so that it will not tip over, you may want to put it on a flat sturdy piece of wood or something similar.
2. Unwrap the whole roll of Wintergreen Lifesavers.® Put the thin straw through all the holes so the candies are all lined up on the straw. You will need to be able to position the straw directly over the mouth of the bottle so that all of the Lifesavers can be dropped into the bottle at the exact same time. **But don't drop them in just yet!**
3. Tell everyone to STAND BACK! After everyone moves back, drop all of the Lifesavers into the bottle at the same time and then move out of the way!!
4. Listen to the oohs and ahhhs!!
5. Repeat the experiment using the diet soda. How is it the same? Different? Does the fountain shoot higher or shorter? Does the soda erupt faster or slower?

Film Canister Pop

Materials

- Film canister (clear is best)
- Water
- Alka-Seltzer® tablets (have lots on hand)
- Some space outside

Caution !

Make sure to aim the film canisters away from children's faces!

Process

1. Do this activity outside at a table.
2. Fill the film canister ¾ full with water.
3. Put the Alka-Seltzer® tablet in the film canister with the water and quickly put the lid back on.
4. Position the film canister in the center of the table.
5. Count out loud together and see how long it takes for the lid to burst off!

Explanation

The carbon dioxide gas formed by the Alka-Seltzer® creates enough pressure to force the top off in a small explosion!

Flame Flattener

Materials

- Votive candle
- Metal pie tin
- Matches
- Measuring cup
- Vinegar (about 3 TBS)
- Baking soda (about 1 TBS)

Process

1. Place candle in center of the pie tin.
2. Put the baking soda into the measuring cup.
3. Slowly pour the vinegar into the baking soda.
4. Wait a few seconds while the mixture begins to bubble.
5. Light the candle.
6. Slowly lift the measuring cup, tilting the spout down toward the flame and make sure the mixture doesn't spill out!
7. Watch as the flame goes out!

Explanation

Carbon dioxide gas is invisible and heavier than air. The flame of the candle (fire) is extinguished by the invisible carbon dioxide gas created by the baking soda and vinegar mixture!

Flame-Resistant Balloon

Materials

- Two large balloons
- Matches
- Water

Note !

This is an experiment that is demonstrated to the children.

Process

1. Blow up one of the balloons and tie a knot in it.
2. Pour ¼ cup of water in the second balloon and tie a knot in it too.
3. Hold the first balloon by the knot. Light a match and hold it under the belly of the balloon try to let the flame touch the rubber. The balloon will pop!
4. Now hold the second balloon. Light a match and hold it under the water in the belly of the balloon. Let the flame touch the rubber. Watch what happens!

Explanation

When the flame touches the balloon without the water, the rubber becomes so hot that it deteriorates and the air inside explodes through. The balloon with the water however does not pop because the water takes on most of the heat instead of the rubber.

Floating Cork

Materials

- A big bowl
- Water
- Corks

Process

1. Fill the bowl half way with water.
2. Put a few corks in the bowl and observe where the corks float.
3. Now fill the bowl to the rim with water, leaving the corks in the water.
4. Where are the corks floating now?

Explanation

Surface tension in the overfilled bowl draws the corks into the center.

Floating Eggs

Materials

- Raw eggs
- Clear plastic party cups
- Water
- Salt (when kosher salt is used, it does not cloud the water like table salt does)

Process

1. Fill the clear cups ¾ full with water.
2. Place an egg into the cup.
3. What happens to the egg??? (It will sink)
4. Now take the egg out and add ½ cup of salt to the water. Stir it up.
5. Put the egg back in. Now what happened? (The egg will float!)

Variation

Try it with a hard boiled egg...
...is it different?

Explanation

Adding salt to the water makes it buoyant enough to hold up the egg.

Flubber

Materials

- 3 TBS Borax
- 1 cup white glue
- 4 cups water
- Food colors or liquid watercolor (if color is desired)
- 2 mixing bowls
- 1 small bowl
- Wooden spoon
- Measuring cups and spoons

Hint

Flubber will keep in an airtight container or Ziploc® for a few weeks. When it begins to flick apart or when it gets too hard, it is time to make a new batch!

Warning: Borax should not be ingested. Try your best to keep this amazing substance off fabric and carpet... but know that VINEGAR does remove it from clothing, carpet and upholstery. Mayonnaise, however, is best to get it out of hair.

Process

1. Mix 2 cups of water and 1 cup of glue in a big bowl.
2. Add color and stir it up.
3. In your smaller bowl, mix together the remaining 2 cups of water and the 3 TBS of Borax. After it's dissolved, pour the Borax mixture slowly and a little at a time into the glue and water mixture and watch it begin to coagulate! Keep pouring (slowly) and mixing at the same time until you create a big flubber ball!
4. **NOTE:** You will not need to use all the Borax water to make your Flubber.

Explanation

Flubber can be classified as a "non-Newtonian fluid." This means it is a substance that has the properties of a solid and liquid at the same time. It feels solid, yet drips through fingers!

Frozen Balloon Blow Up

Materials

- Warm water (about 4 cups)
- Glass bottle
- Round balloon
- Pie tin
- Freezer

Process

1. Put the bottle in the freezer for at least 1-2 hours.
2. Stretch the balloon by blowing it up so that it is ready to expand (but let the air out).
3. Remove the bottle from the freezer and attach the balloon over the mouth.
4. Place the bottle in the center of the pie tin.
5. Pour the warm water into the pie tin, surrounding the base of the glass bottle.
6. Watch the balloon blow up by itself.

Explanation

The bottle was very cold so the air inside was very compact. When warm water was added the air began to heat up and expand into the balloon.

Heat Rises

Materials

- Large clear plastic bowl
- Baby food jar with lid that has a small hole in it
- Food color
- Cold water
- Hot water

Process

1. Fill a large plastic bowl 2/3 full with cold water.
2. Fill the baby food jar with hot water and add a few drops of food coloring.
3. Put the lid on and submerge the baby food jar into the bowl of cold water.
4. Observe what happens to the colored water.

Explanation

Heat rises. The hot colored water rises to the surface as it escapes.

Hovercraft

Materials

- 1 large balloon, 9 or 11 inch size
- 1 "pull-open-push-close" top (found on most liquid dish soap bottles)
- A CD you have no intention of ever using again
- Hot glue gun
- A smooth flat surface

Hint

This experiment makes one hovercraft. I suggest having one hovercraft for each child!

Variation

Once the children get the hang of it you can have races! Chart and graph results to deepen this experiment and expand it into your math curriculum!

Process

1. Prior to the experiment, hot glue the plastic top onto the CD, centering it over the hole in the middle of the disc. Wait 24 hours for the glue to dry.
2. Make sure the "pull-open-push-close" top is in the "closed" position when you get started.
3. Blow up the balloon.
4. Put the inflated balloon over the plastic top (still in the "closed" position).
5. Carefully pull open the plastic top to release the air from the balloon and watch the disc glide across the flat surface.

Explanation

The released air from the balloon pushes down through the opening in the disc, creating a cushion of air under the disc which allows it to glide across the flat surface.

Ice Mountain

Materials

- Sensory Tub
- Ice cubes
- Large bowls
- Food coloring or liquid watercolor – you can focus on the primaries here: red, yellow and blue
- Rock salt
- Eye droppers or pipettes
- Small cups to hold the coloring

Variation

A BLOCK of ice can be used instead of the ice cubes.

Process

1. Empty a TON of ice cubes into some large bowls and re-freeze them. This will become the ice mountain.
2. When you are ready to do the project, empty the frozen mountain into your sensory tub.
3. Sprinkle rock salt all over the ice mountain – allow it to sit for a few minutes before beginning to color it.
4. Use the pipettes and colored water to drop the colors over the ice mountain and into the holes created by the rock salt!

Explanation

By mixing primary colors (red, blue and yellow) you make the secondary colors (orange, green and purple).

Also, salt lowers the freezing point of ice, causing it to melt. The large chunks of rock salt then create the big holes that the children enjoy poking colors into!

Jumping Spices

Materials

- Salt and coarsely ground pepper
- Balloons (1 for each child)
- Pie tin

Variation

Can the balloon lift up some Rice Krispies®?

Provide a mirror so that children can watch their hair stand up once it has been "charged" by the balloons.

Try to stick the "charged" balloons on the wall.

Process

1. Sprinkle both salt and pepper onto the pie tin.
2. Rub the inflated balloon through your hair to gather static electricity.
3. Hold the balloon over the salt and pepper.

Explanation

Static electricity is produced by rubbing two things together. The balloon becomes "charged" after being run through your hair and the salt and pepper are attracted to it.

Lava Light

Materials

- Plastic cup for each child
- Salt
- Water
- Oil
- Liquid watercolor

Process

1. Fill the plastic cups 1/3 of the way with water.
2. Add about an inch of oil to the cups. Watch as the oil stays on the top of the water.
3. Slowly drip drop 3-5 drops of coloring into the cup and notice how the color stays in the oil.
4. Pour a little salt into the oil/water mixture and sit back and enjoy the show!
5. This experiment can be done over and over by adding more salt.

Explanation

The concept of density is at work here. Water is heavier (more dense) than the oil, but the salt is heavier than the oil and the water! As the salt sinks, the oil clings to it and sinks too. When the salt begins to dissolve the oil is released and it floats back up to the top.

Lifting Ice

Materials

- 2 small cups for each child
- Water
- Ice cubes
- Salt
- Cotton string cut into 3 inch sections. Have at least 1 for each child and always make extras!

Process

1. Partially fill cup #1 with some water. Put an ice cube in cup #2.
2. Make sure each child has a piece of string.
3. Moisten the string in the cup of water.
4. Place the string on top of the ice.
5. Sprinkle salt onto the ice cube and string.
6. Count to ten and gently lift the string.

Variation

Try to lift an ice cube with just the string without using the salt. Does it work?

Explanation

Salt lowers the freezing point of ice, causing it to melt. Water appears on top of the ice cube and the string sinks into the water. As the ice cube melts the salt and water mixture is diluted and the freezing point goes up. The ice refreezes trapping the string inside the ice cube and allowing the children to lift the ice cube!

Magic Drawing

Materials

- Baking soda
- Water
- White copy paper
- Grape juice
- Cups to hold the "magic mixture" of baking soda/water
- Cups to hold the grape juice
- Paint brushes

Process

1. Mix a solution of 1/4 cup baking soda to 1 cup water.
2. Draw a picture or design with the baking soda solution on the white paper.
3. Let the paper dry completely. It will appear blank.
4. Pour the grape juice into a small cup. Use a paint brush to paint over the paper with the grape juice.
5. What happened?

Note !

Be sure to make a batch of the baking soda and water solution and try the experiment out beforehand to be sure you'll have enough for all your children!

Explanation

Grape juice is your indicator. Baking soda is a base (alkaline). When an alkaline substance is added to an indicator liquid a greenish-blue color will "magically" appear!

Magic Touch Bags

Materials

- 5 TBS Cornstarch
- ½ cup water
- ½ cup oil
- Large Ziploc® bags
- Liquid watercolor
- Masking tape

Hint

To save: Use clothespins to hang your magic touch bags from your drying rack!

Process

1. In a large Ziploc® bag mix the cornstarch, water and a few drops of color. (Make sure the ingredients are well combined.)
2. Add the oil.
3. Seal the bag, making sure to get all the air out, and place it flat on the table. Masking tape the edges down onto the table.
4. Let the children push and play with the bags flat on the table.
5. Watch the mixture change both when you play with it and when you let it rest.

Explanation

Because the oil and cornstarch mixture will mix and then separate, the combination of these ingredients makes for an interesting mixture visual and tactile sensory exploration.

Magnifying Bucket

Materials

- 2½ gallon plastic ice cream bucket
- Plastic wrap
- 2 large rubber bands
- X-ACTO® knife, box cutter or a very sharp pair of scissors
- Water
- An assortment of small goodies to examine through the magnifying bucket

Note !

You make the bucket. The children will use the bucket

Explanation

The plastic wrap and water combine to form a convex lens which provides magnification.

Process

To make it:

1. Using the X-ACTO®, sharp scissors or box cutter, carefully cut a large hole in one side of the bucket that is close to the bottom. When cutting the hole remember it will need to be big enough to fit hands through!

To use it:

1. Place clear plastic wrap on top of the bucket. The wrap should be a little loose across the top of the bucket - not stretched tight.
2. Place the large rubber bands around the top of the bucket to hold the plastic wrap in place. Check to make sure that the plastic is secure around the entire top of the bucket.
3. Pour water onto the top of the plastic wrap. The plastic keeps the water from going into the bucket.
5. The children then can place the object they wish to magnify into the bucket through the hole in the side. Look down through the water on top of the plastic wrap to see that the object is magnified!

Hint

Instead of a rubber band, masking tape can be used to secure the plastic wrap.

Make a Cloud

Materials

- 2 liter bottle (with a top)
- Water
- Matches

Process

1. Pour about 2 inches of HOT tap water into the bottle (the hotter the better).
2. Blow a big puff of air into the bottle and close the lid quickly and securely.
3. Take turns shaking the bottle.
4. Have the children stand back and watch as you light a match. Open the top of the bottle and drop the match in. Close the bottle as quickly as possible.
5. Place the bottle on its side and squeeze the bottle as hard as you can. Then release. Continue to squeeze and release until a cloud forms in the bottle.
6. When you see the cloud, take off the cap and let the cloud go. You may need to squeeze the bottle to get it out.

Explanation

When you shake the bottle, water molecules are circulated evenly throughout the air in the bottle. When you add the smoke from the match and the pressure from squeezing the bottle, you have created the perfect atmosphere for a cloud. The water molecules stuck to the smoke particles in the air and created a cloud!

Marble Racing

Materials

- Marbles
- 4 jars of the same size
- Honey
- Corn syrup
- Water
- Cooking oil

Variation

Try out other liquids and see what happens when you drop marbles in. Drop a button or a Lego® block and see if the outcome is the same or different.

Process

1. Fill the jars with equal amounts of liquids: one with oil, one with honey, one with corn syrup and one with water.
2. Place the jars with oil and honey next to each other. Place the jars with corn syrup and water next to each other.
3. Have one child hold a marble over the oil while another child holds the marble over the honey.
4. On the count of three, the children should drop their marbles simultaneously into the jar while all members of the group watch carefully to see which marble reaches the bottom of the jar first.
5. Repeat the process with corn syrup and water.
6. Repeat the experiment with additional marbles and see if the outcome is the same.

Explanation

The degree to which a fluid resists flow when force is applied is called viscosity. A highly viscous liquid is one that flows slowly. Objects move slowly through a highly viscous liquid.

Metal Chimes

Materials

- A variety of metal objects: spoons, trivets, baking trays, coat hangers, slinkies, etc.
- Cotton string

Process

1. Attach a piece of cotton string to one end of each of the metal objects.
2. Hold the string with your hand and swing the spoon or hanger so that it taps a hard object such as the back of a chair, the floor, the table top, the side of the table, the wall... etc. What does it sound like?
3. Swing the object again, but this time instead of just holding the string, wind the string around your finger a couple of times and place your finger up near your ear!
4. Tap various surfaces again. Now what do you hear?
5. How are the sounds same and different?

Explanation

Metal vibrates when it strikes an object. The vibrations travel up the string to the ears where the sound is amplified.

Mini Balloon Pump

Materials

- Large round balloon
- Plastic bottle (Windex® bottles work the best)

Process

1. Make sure the bottle is clean and dry.
2. Attach the balloon to the mouth of the bottle. (You may want to pull and stretch the balloon first so that it expands easier).
3. Let the children squeeze the bottle to inflate the balloon.

Explanation

By squeezing the bottle the air is forced to move into the balloon, which expands with the pressure.

Mini Magnifier

Materials

- Pieces of cardboard (approximately 3 x 6 inches)
- Small pieces of plastic wrap (approximately 2 x 3 inches)
- Tape
- Eye droppers or pipettes
- Small paper cups containing water
- Variety of small objects to examine with the magnifier

Process

1. Prior to the experiment cut out enough 3x6 cardboard squares for each child. Cut a 1x1 inch opening in the middle of each piece of cardboard.
2. Tape the plastic wrap over the 1x1 opening creating a plastic wrap "window."
3. Put a few drops of water on to the plastic wrap and hold the magnifier over small objects and see what happens!

Explanation

The wrap and the water combine to form a convex lens which provides magnification.

Mixing Colors

Materials

- Baby food jars
- Water
- Eye droppers or pipettes
- Food coloring or liquid watercolor
  – red, yellow and blue for this one!

Process

1. Fill some baby food jars with red water, yellow water and blue water. Have some jars available with NON-COLORED water and have some available with NO water at all.
2. Allow some free flowing explorations of color mixing using the colored water and the eye droppers.

Explanation

By mixing primary colors (red, blue and yellow) you can make the secondary colors (orange, green and purple).

Moving Toothpicks

Materials

- Dish pan bucket (small sensory tub)
- Sugar cube
- Water
- Small chunk of soap
- 6 toothpicks

Process

1. Fill the dish pan bucket about halfway.
2. Have the children place the toothpicks in the center of the pan in a circle.
3. Place a sugar cube in the middle of the toothpicks and watch what happens!
4. Dump out the water and try again. This time place the piece of soap in the middle and watch what happens.

Explanation

This is an example of surface tension. The sugar cube sucked up the water and pulled the toothpicks towards the center of the pan, whereas the soap's film spread out and pushes the toothpicks towards the sides of the pan. In both cases the surface tension on the water acts like an invisible skin, when the sugar and soap were added, the skin was broken.

Musical Bottles

Materials

- Various sizes of glass bottles
- Food coloring or liquid watercolors
- Water
- Metal spoons

Process

1. Fill the bottles with water of varying amounts.
2. Color the water in each bottle to provide variety and distinction.
3. Arrange the bottles in a row, and have children gently tap the top of the bottles with the spoons to make different sounds.
4. Rearrange the bottles and repeat the process to hear the different sounds.

Explanation

There is a different amount of air in each bottle, so each one makes a different sound when tapped with the spoon.

No Pop Balloon Pop

Materials

- Balloons
- Pin or safety pin
- Different kinds of tape:
  packing, masking,
  electrical, duct, scotch, etc.

Process

1. Blow up some balloons and demonstrate how a pin will POP the balloon.
2. Is there a way to get the air out of a balloon without popping it?? YES!
3. Blow up another balloon.
4. Place two strips of tape, forming an "X," on the balloon.
5. Use a pin to poke a hole in the tape at the center of the "X".
6. What is happening? Put your hands over the hole in the balloon to feel the air coming out.

Variation

Put the taped side of the punctured balloon into a pan of water. Watch as the bubbles of air escape from the deflating balloon. Which kind of tape worked best?

Explanation

The tape prevents the balloon from splitting apart at the puncture.

Noisy Peas

Materials

- 1 lb. dried peas
- Wine glass
- Water
- Pie tin

Process

1. Place the wine glass in the center of the pie tin.
2. Fill the wine glass completely with the peas.
3. Pour water into the wine glass up to the brim.
4. Let peas absorb water over the next hour or so while you continue to periodically add water allowing the peas to swell.
5. Watch and listen as the peas begin to expand and fall over the side of the glass and into the metal tin!

Explanation

The peas absorb the water through the tiny holes in their skin. The peas expand making them too big for the glass and then they fall out of the glass and onto the pie tin where they make a "tink tink" sound on the tin!

Oil and Water Art

Materials

- White coffee filters
- Water
- Shallow baking pans or water table
- Cooking oil in a squeeze bottle
- Clothespins
- Liquid watercolor or food coloring

Process

1. Place an inch of water in each pan or water table.
2. Add some color to the water.
3. Now squeeze some oil into the water.
4. Give each child a coffee filter and two clothespins. Have them attach a clothespin on either side of the filter to make handles.
5. Dip the filters into the water and slowly pull them out.
6. Observe what happened to the filters once they dried!

Explanation

The colored water and oil do not mix and this creates the colored designs and patterns on the coffee filter.

Ooblick - A Sensational Suspension

Materials

- 6 cups of cornstarch (at least)
- 6 cups of water (at least)
- Liquid watercolor or food coloring (optional)
- Wooden spoon
- Sensory tub
- Pitcher to hold the water

Process

1. Dump the cornstarch into your sensory tub.
2. Slowly add the water and mix well – sometimes you need all the water and sometimes you don't. Don't just dump all the water in at once! You could very well ruin the batch! Go slow! The mixture will be stiff and hard at first but keep working with it.
3. Add a few drops of coloring if desired.
4. Scoop the mixture up with your hands! Watch it turn from a solid into a liquid right before your eyes!

Note !

The basic ratio for a successful batch of ooblick is one part cornstarch to one part water.

Explanation

The cornstarch and water mix together but do not dissolve. This is called a suspension. Moving and squeezing the substance keeps the suspension together. When the action stops the material is no longer held in a suspension and it feels like a liquid substance. The big 50 cent word for a suspension is a Non-Newtonian fluid.

Over the Brim

Materials

- Clear plastic party cups - 1 for each child
- Pennies (25 - 30 per child)
- Water

Process

1. Fill the cups completely full with water.
2. Slowly slip the pennies into the water ONE AT A TIME
3. Watch as the water level rises above the brim of the cup without spilling out.
4. How many pennies will it take before the water spills out??

Explanation

Surface tension allows the water to bulge above the brim of the cup.

Oxygen Deprived Candle

Materials

- Votive candle
- Pie pan
- Food coloring or liquid watercolors
- Different sized jars

Process

1. Fill a pie tin with about ½ inch of water.
2. Place a few drops of color in it. (Color makes it easier for the children to see what is happening).
3. Place a candle in the middle of the pie pan and light it.
4. Place a jar over the candle and have children observe what happens (The candle will go out and water level will rise in the jar).
5. Try this again using different size jars. Count aloud how many seconds it takes for the candle to go out in the different jars.

Variation

Have someone blow into one of the jars and then repeat experiment to see if blowing into the jar changes the amount of time it takes for the candle to extinguish.

Explanation

It takes oxygen for a flame to burn. When the oxygen is used up inside the jar the flame is extinguished. This creates a vacuum which forces the water to rise inside the jar.

Paper Holds Water

Materials

- Small cups
- Water
- 3 x 5 index cards or playing cards

Process

1. Fill the cup halfway with water.
2. Place an index or playing card over the rim of the cup. Press down hard to make a tight seal.
3. With one hand on the card and one hand holding the cup, quickly turn the cup upside down and hold it in mid-air.
4. Continue to hold the cup upside down but remove your hand from the card.
5. The card will remain sealed on the cup and the water will stay inside the cup! Amazing!

Caution !

The seal will weaken after awhile, and the water will spill out. Do this experiment over a water table tub, a towel or the grass!

Explanation

There is more air pressure outside the cup than inside the cup, so even when upside down the water stays in the jar.

Variation

Instead of using a cup, use a bottle with a small mouth. After the bottle is filled with water, cover the mouth of the bottle with a piece of index card that is cut a little larger than the bottle opening. Make sure there is a good seal before turning the bottle upside down.

Peppy Paprika

Materials

- Shallow dish – 9x13 baking pan, water table tub, pie tin... whatever you got!
- Water
- Dishwashing liquid – ¼ cup will be plenty
- Toothpicks
- Sugar – have 1 cup of it on hand
- Paprika

Hint

You may have to add more sugar to larger dishes of water in order to be able to repeat the process!

Variation

Try pepper instead of paprika.

Process

1. Fill your dish ¾ full with water.
2. Sprinkle paprika on the surface of the water.
3. Dip the tip of a toothpick into the dish soap.
4. Now touch the paprika with the soapy toothpick and observe what happens to the paprika!
5. By stirring 1 TBS of sugar into the water you can repeat the process over again!

Explanation

The surface tension is broken by touching the water with dishwashing liquid. The sugar helps restore the surface tension so that the experiment can be repeated.

Rainbow Layers

Materials

- Plastic cups
- Green colored water
- Blue dish soap
- Cooking oil
- Pink shampoo

Process

1. Pour each of the ingredients into a cup, one at a time and in any order.
2. Watch as the layers begin to separate.
3. Once they have separated repeat the experiment but this time pour the ingredients into a cup in a different order.
4. See if the layers end up the same!

Explanation

All of the ingredients are of a different density. No matter which order you pour them into the cup they will always separate out the same.

Raining Color

Materials

- Large mouth mason jar
- Water
- Food coloring or liquid watercolors
- Toothpicks

Process

1. Fill the mason jar 1/3 full with water.
2. Pour a layer of oil on top of the water.
3. Drip drop a few drops of coloring into the oil – they will float on the oil.
4. Using the tip of the toothpick, carefully push the droplet of color through the layer of oil until it reaches the water.
5. Notice that once the color droplet reaches the water it bursts and rains down through the water!

Explanation

Oil and water do not mix. The color droplet is soluble in water but not in oil. The color will remain as a droplet in the oil but will mix with the water after being pushed through the layer of oil.

Rising Balls

Materials

- Rice
- Small balls (golf or ping-pong balls work the best)
- A wide mouth jar with a lid

Process

1. Place the balls in the jar.
2. Let the children pour rice into the jar, but leave about 2 inches at the top.
3. Place the lid on the jar, and give each child a turn at shaking the jar back and forth from side to side.
4. Watch as the balls rise to the top of the jar.

Explanation

The rice is heavier than the balls. So, as you shake the jar, the rice settles to the bottom and the balls are forced to rise to the top.

Rising Water

Materials

- Clear plastic tube, 18 inches long and 3/8 inch in diameter
- Pie tin
- Large clear jar (32 oz.)
- Food coloring or liquid watercolor
- Straws
- Water

Note !

I suggest having more than one of these contraptions out and available for the children, along with a hefty supply of replacement straws so everyone can take many turns!

Process

1. Fill the pie tin with 1 inch of colored water.
2. Turn the jar upside down and place it in the middle of the pie tin.
3. Tilt the jar to one side and insert one end of the tubing into the jar. Push the tubing in until it almost touches the top of the jar. The rest of the tube will extend out of the jar and over the edge of the pie tin.

FYI: The jar may need to be steadied by an adult because it will be wobbly when it rests on the tubing.

4. Push a plastic straw into the exposed tubing.
5. Demonstrate how you can fill the jar with the colored water by inhaling through the straw.

Explanation

When the air in the jar is removed (sucked out via the straw) you have created a vacuum. The vacuum forces the water level to rise inside the jar.

Rolling Penny

Materials

- A penny for each child
- A large balloon for each child (the clear ones are great so you can see what's going on inside!)

Process

1. Push the penny all the way through the mouth of the balloon.
2. Blow up the balloon and tie it closed. Make sure not to over inflate the balloon or it might pop!
3. Hold the balloon upside down at the tie and rapidly rotate the balloon in a circular motion until the penny begins to spin. Although it may bounce at first, if you hold the balloon parallel to the ground it should roll along the inside of the balloon with ease.
4. Stop the rotation of the balloon with your other hand and watch what happens to the penny!

Explanation

The balloon is inflicting an inward force on the penny and because of that force the penny rotates in a circular motion, even when the balloon stops moving. This is an example of centrifugal force.

Rubber Egg

 ## Materials

- Raw egg
- Jar
- Vinegar

 ## Process

1. Place the raw egg in the jar.
2. Pour vinegar into the jar until the egg is completely covered.
3. Let contents sit for 48 hours.
4. Carefully remove the egg from the jar.
5. Gently explore the outer surface of the egg!

Caution !

If the membrane is broken, the egg will pop like an egg filled balloon!

Variation

Coat one half of the eggshell with fluoride toothpaste before placing the egg in vinegar. The fluoride coated side will not dissolve as completely as the uncoated side! The fluoride prevents the calcium in the eggshell from completely dissolving in the vinegar.

 ## Explanation

Vinegar dissolves the calcium in the eggshell but the egg continues to be held together by its membrane.

Secret Solution

Materials

- Large clear plastic party cups
- 7-up®
- Blueberry syrup
- Heavy cream

Process

1. Pour the following liquids into the cup:
   2 inches of 7-Up® (Cherry flavored 7-Up® works well for additional color contrast)
   ½ inch of blueberry syrup
   1 inch of cream
2. Notice that the liquid remained in three separate layers!

Explanation

Each of the three liquids has a different density so they remain separate layers when poured into the same cup.

Seeing Sound

Materials

- Tuning forks (available at music stores)
- Water tub
- Water

Process

1. Tap the tuning fork on the edge of a table and then place the vibrating fork into the water.
2. Watch the water dance!

Explanation

When you tap the tuning fork on the table you are creating sound vibrations which you can hear. By placing the tuning fork in the water you are able to actually see them! The sound vibrations move through the water and become visible to the eye.

Shiny Pennies

Materials

- 2 pennies per child
- Baby food jars – 1 for each child
- ¼ cup vinegar
- 1 tsp salt
- Plastic spoons – 1 for each child

Process

1. Have children mix the vinegar and salt in their individual baby food jars.
2. Now put the pennies in the jar.
3. Watch the changes taking place as they stir the pennies in their jar!

Explanation

The salt and vinegar combine to make a strong acid which cleans the dirt off the pennies.

Shrinking Letters

Materials

- Balloon for each child
- Permanent markers
- String

Process

1. Give each child an inflated balloon that has been tied with a string - not the standard knot!
2. Use the markers to write, draw or scribble on the balloons.
3. Untie the string on the balloon. Their drawings and letters will shrink and become much darker as the balloon deflates.
4. Blow it up again and watch them g-r-o-w!

Explanation

When the surface size of the balloon shrinks so does the printed image.

Silly Sippers

Materials

- Baby food jars – one for each child
- Water
- Straws – enough for each child to have 2

Process

1. Pour water into the baby food jars.
2. Put a straw in water and sip.
3. Now place the other straw so it is outside of the glass.
4. Have children sip through both straws at the same time (one in the water – one not)
5. Notice what happened!

Variation

Using only one straw, cut a small notch in the straw about one inch from the top. Have the children try to sip the water. What happened? Why?

Explanation

The straw on the outside of the glass lets in air! Because of this, the students cannot create the vacuum which is necessary to sip the water through the other straw.

Silly Sound Makers

Materials

- A variety of recycled containers – ice cream pints, popcorn bucket, oatmeal canister, small paper cups or even plastic yogurt containers.
- Pieces of cotton string cut 12-18 inches long
- Toothpick
- Small piece of sponge

Hint

Different sized containers will make different sounds.

Explanation

Friction causes vibrations to move along the string and vibrate on the bottom of the cup, making the silly sounds!

Process

1. Poke a hole in the bottom of the container.
2. Tie the string around the middle of a toothpick.
3. Turning the container so it is upside down, thread the toothpick with the string through the hole. The toothpick will prevent the string from being pulled out.
4. Keep the container upside down, so that the string will dangle down from the bottom.
5. Dampen the small piece of sponge.
6. Grasping the container in one hand and the sponge in the other, pinch the sponge around the dangling string.
7. Gripping tightly, pull the sponge down the string to make a silly sound!

Slime Test

Materials

- Water
- Liquid soap
- Cooking oil
- 5 bowls
- Lots of Jell-O® squares
  (enough for all your children
  to do the activity 5 times)

Explanation

Lubricants are used for many different things in our world. They help to decrease friction between two objects. The oil, water and soap acted as lubricants for the children's fingers.

Process

The Set Up:
The idea here is that the children will notice how different lubricants make objects slippery. By having "relays" with Jell-O® squares covered in various substances they will be able to see that some lubricants are more effective than others.

You will have 4 bowls of Jell-O® squares and one empty bucket.

Bowl #1 – plain (non coated) Jell-O® squares
Bowl #2 – Jell-O® squares coated in ¼ cup of liquid dish soap
Bowl #3 – Jell-O® squares coated in ¼ cup water
Bowl #4 – Jell-O® squares coated in ¼ cup oil
Bowl #5 (the Dump Bucket) needs to be a container big enough to hold all the Jell-O® which will be transferred into it! Maybe your sensory tub? Make sure you have the dump bucket at least 12 inches (1 foot) away from the other four bowls.

The Actual Process:
1. Take turns transferring the Jell-O® WITH YOUR FINGERS from the various bowls into the Dump Bucket. Do one bowl at a time so the children can really feel the difference between the various coatings.

2. Be sure to wash hands between bowls!

3. After all the Jell-O® has been transferred, discuss which was the best lubricant (the most slippery) and which was the worst (least slippery). Chart your findings!

Soap Boat

Materials

- 1 Index card
- Large tub or pan
- Liquid soap
- Scissors

Process

1. Cut the index card to look like a boat by making a triangle 2 ½ inches long and 1 ½ inches wide. Cut out a small notch on the back (across from the point).
2. Fill the tub with water.
3. Place the "boat" in the water and pour a small amount of soap into the notch.
4. Watch as the boat speeds across the water!

Explanation

By adding the soap the surface tension of the water was broken and it propelled the boat forward with the current.

Sound Makers

Materials

- 3-5 plastic eggs
- Small items to put inside: rice, beans, paperclips, coins, sand, etc.

Process

1. Mark each egg with a number.
2. Fill each egg with different materials. One with rice, one with beans, etc...
3. Close the eggs and let the children shake each egg and try to guess what's inside. Write the guesses down on a large sheet of paper.
4. After talking about the guesses open the eggs and show the children what each egg contained.
5. Repeat the process.

Explanation

By shaking the eggs, sound waves were produced. When you listen carefully, your brain is able to determine all kinds of different sounds. Even the subtle sound differences inside the eggs are enough to allow you to identify the objects.

Spinning Eggs

Materials

- Raw eggs
- Hard boiled eggs
- Clear cups

Process

1. Crack open the raw egg and put it into a clear cup to see.
2. Crack a hard boiled egg and put it into a clear cup as well.
3. Discuss their similarities and differences.
4. Put the cups aside.
5. Spin a hard boiled egg and a raw one at the same time.
6. Notice the differences and try to identify which is which.

Explanation

The cooked egg spins evenly and with more speed than the raw egg. The cooked egg can even be spun in a vertical position (on its end). It is solid with a specific center of gravity.

The raw egg has fluid contents which shift during the spinning process. This causes the egg to spin unevenly. Spin the eggs again. Gently stop each egg by touching it briefly. When you remove your finger the raw egg continues to wobble while the cooked egg remains still. Why?

Strength Test

Materials

- Eggs
- Water tub or bucket (in case they break)

Process

1. Pick up an egg.
2. Hold your hand over the water tub or bucket just in case the egg breaks!
3. Place the egg in the palm of your hand.
4. Close your fingers around the egg and squeeze the egg as hard as you can.
5. What happened?

Explanation

When you crack an egg you tap it on the corner of a sharp surface to break it. However, when you squeeze an egg, the force and pressure of your squeeze is being spread out over the whole surface of the eggshell and therefore doesn't break!

T-Shirt Science

Materials

- Pre-washed white t-shirt
- Sharpie® Permanent Markers in various colors (Red, Orange, Yellow, Green, Blue, Purple, Black)
- Plastic cups to hold the rubbing alcohol
- Rubber bands
- Rubbing alcohol
- Pipettes or eyedroppers
- Various cylindrical containers from snacks such as peanuts, chips, pretzels, etc...

Explanation

This is a lesson in the concepts of solubility, color mixing, and the movement of molecules. Sharpie® markers contain permanent ink, which will not wash away with water. However, the molecules of ink will wash away with another liquid – rubbing alcohol. Rubbing alcohol acts as a solvent and moves the different colors of ink with it as it spreads throughout the fabric.

Process

1. Lay the shirt flat on the table.
2. Place the snack canister inside the shirt with the opening directly under the section of the shirt that you want to decorate. Stretch a rubber band over the t-shirt and canister to secure the shirt in place.
3. Use the permanent markers to make designs and patterns on the section of fabric which is stretched out over the canister.
4. Using the pipettes, drip drop rubbing alcohol into the center of the design you made with the markers.
5. Apply as much or as little rubbing alcohol as desired, but try not to drench your shirt!
6. Remove the rubber band, reposition the canister, and move on to decorate a new area of the shirt!

Caution !

Rubbing alcohol is flammable and must be kept away from any open flames or heat. This experiment must be conducted in a well ventilated area, preferably outdoors!

Note !

You can set the colors by placing the shirt in the laundry dryer for approximately 15 minutes after the ink is dry.

Telephone

Materials

- 2, 8 oz. containers (yogurt containers work just fine!)
- 4 foot piece of cotton string
- Toothpicks

Process

1. Poke a hole in the bottom of each yogurt cup.
2. Thread the ends of the string up through the bottom of each yogurt cup.
3. Tie each end of the string around the toothpicks and pull the string tight between each cup. Make sure that the toothpick is in the bottom of each cup.
4. Have the children work in pairs.
5. Give each child one cup. Have one child talk into the cup while the other listens. Make sure that they keep the string tight between each other.

Variation

Tin cans can be used instead of yogurt cup but be sure that no sharp edges are exposed.

Explanation

Sound waves travel along the string. The sound is amplified by the cups.

Temperature Confusion

Materials

- 3 large bowls
- Water
- Towels

Process

1. Fill one bowl with ice water, one bowl with room temperature water, and one bowl with very warm water.
2. Have a child put both hands into the room temperature water.
3. Then put one hand in the ice water and one hand in the very warm water at the same time.
4. Leave hands in the water for about 3 seconds.
5. Have the child put both hands back into the room temperature water.
6. Ask the child how each hand feels.

Explanation

The hand in the warm water has become used to feeling warmth, so it feels cooled in the room temperature water. The hand in the cold water has become used to feeling cold, so it feels warmed by the room temperature water. This is called sensory adaptation. Dramatic changes can fool the sense receptors and send confusing messages to the brain.

Temperature Mixing

Materials

- 4 empty baby food jars
- Hot water (colored red)
- Cold water (colored blue)
- 2 separate 3x5 index cards

Note !

This is an experiment that is demonstrated to the children.

Process

1. Fill each of the jars to the brim, two with the red hot water, and two with the blue cold water.
2. Place an index card over the mouth of one of the blue cold water jars. Hold the card in place as you flip the jar upside down and rest it on top of one of the red hot water jars. Make sure they are lined up mouth to mouth.
3. Hold the jar on top in place as you gently remove the index card from between the two jars. What happened? (The colors should have mixed to make purple water!)
4. Repeat the experiment but this time put the red hot water on top of the blue cold water!
5. What happened this time? (The red water should remain on the top and the blue water should remain on the bottom. The water should not mix when the hot water is on the top.)

Explanation

This is an experiment in density and temperature. Hot water is lighter (less dense) than cold water. When you have cold water on the top and remove the 3x5 card, the cold water (denser and heavier) will sink to the bottom of the jars. The hot water (less dense and lighter) will rise to the top and consequently the colors mix to make a jar full of purple water. However, when you put the hot water on top and remove the 3x5 card barrier, the hot water is trapped at the top (because it is lighter and less dense) and is unable to move. When the hot water is on the top the colors will not mix.

Time Warp Hose

Materials

- Long garden hose

Process

1. Coil the hose and have a child hold both ends of the hose.
2. Have the child place one end near one ear while speaking into the other end.

Explanation

There is a delay in the time the sound is made and the time it is received by the ear.

Water Magic

Materials

- A tall glass with a rounded edge – a mayonnaise jar works well!
- Water
- A handkerchief

Note !

This is an experiment that is demonstrated to the children.

Process

1. Place the handkerchief over the glass. Push some of the handkerchief into the opening of the jar. Hold the rest of the handkerchief around the sides of the jar with your hands.
2. Fill the glass with water (through the handkerchief) until it's about ¾ full.
3. Now stretch the handkerchief carefully down the sides of the glass so that it is very tight across the top. With one hand, hold the edges of the handkerchief tightly around the sides of the glass.
4. Place your free hand over the mouth of the glass and quickly turn the glass upside down.
5. Remove your hand from the mouth of the glass and watch as the water stays in the jar!

Explanation

By stretching the handkerchief you are creating surface tension. Water molecules are too small to break that tension. If you touch the handkerchief while it is upside down, the tension would be broken and the water will come through! Try it over a bucket (or the lawn) to see!

Yeast Inflated Balloon

Materials

- A small bottle with narrow neck
- Pitcher of warm water
- 1 Balloon
- 1 Packet of yeast
- 1 TBS sugar
- Time!

Process

1. Place the sugar in the bottle.
2. Pour water into the bottle until it is about 1/3 full.
3. Add the package of dry yeast to the bottle and mix.
4. Stretch mouth of balloon over the top of the bottle.
5. Keep an eye on the balloon and bottle for the next hour as this experiment takes 30 – 40 minutes.

Explanation

Yeast consumes the sugar and creates carbon dioxide gas. As the carbon dioxide is released, the balloon inflates.

Zoom Zoom Balloon

Materials

- Plastic straw
- Long balloon (Round doesn't work as well)
- A long stretch of string
- Tape
- Paperclip
- Two chairs

Process

1. Blow up the balloon and use the paperclip to keep it closed.
2. Thread the string through the straw.
3. Carefully (yet securely) tape the balloon to the straw.
4. Tape the two ends of the string to the chairs. Make sure the string is nice and tight!
5. Move the balloon to one end of the string. Be sure to have the balloon positioned correctly so the air will zoom out the back of the balloon and propel it down the length of the string when you take off the paperclip.
6. Remove the paperclip and watch the balloon zoom!

Explanation

Every action has an equal and opposite reaction. As the air blew out of the back of the balloon, it forced the balloon to move in the opposite direction.

The End Stuff

Glossary

Absorb

To take in and soak up through pores or tiny openings.

Absorbent

Able to retain all that which has been taken in.

Acid

Acids are characterized by their sour taste. Acids react with and dissolve certain metals to form salts. The first precise definition of an acid and base was given by Svante Arrhenius, and is referred to as Arrhenius Theory. An acid is any substance that would turn a litmus indicator red. When cabbage juice is used as the indicator, acids turn the juice pink. Common household acids are: lemon juice, vinegar and soda pop.

Action

A physical change, as in position, mass or energy, that an object or system undergoes.

Agitate

To move with sudden forcefulness; irregular or rapid action.

Air Pressure

The push of air on all surfaces. The pressure exerted by the movement of molecules in the atmosphere.

Alkali

Soluble mineral salts typically found in natural water and arid soils. A substance that contains an alkali would be called alkaline.

Amplify

To make larger or greater in amount or intensity.

Arid

Lacking moisture because of insufficient rainfall; dry.

Atmosphere

The envelope of gas that surrounds the earth (or any celestial body) and is retained by such body's gravitational field.

Atom

The smallest unit of matter.

Base

Bases, or alkaline substances, are characterized by their bitter taste and slippery feel. They react with acids to form salts. The first precise definition of an acid and base was given by Svante Arrhenius, and is referred to as Arrhenius Theory. A base is any substance that would turn a litmus indicator blue. When cabbage juice is used as the indicator, bases turn the juice green. Common household bases are: ammonia, laundry detergent and baking soda.

Buoyant

Capable of floating.

Buoyancy

The tendency to remain afloat in a liquid or to rise in air or gas. It is also the upward force that a fluid exerts on an object less dense than itself.

Calcium

A moderately hard metallic element. It is a basic component of bone, shells and leaves and constitutes approximately 3% of the earth's crust.

Capillaries

A tube with a small internal diameter.

Carbon Dioxide

A colorless, odorless, incombustible (not capable of burning) gas.

Center of Gravity

The point at which all the mass of an object seems to be focused.

Centrifugal Force

The force on a body that is directed away from the center of circular rotation.

Centripetal Force

The force on a body that is directed towards the center of circular rotation.

Charge

When an object is "charged," tiny particles called electrons move from one object to the other leaving both with an electrical charge. These charges have been arbitrarily designated as positive and negative.

Chemical Reaction

A chemical change in which one or more different kinds of matter are formed.

Circumference

The distance around a circle or sphere.

Coagulant

Any agent that causes coagulation.

Coagulate

To transform a liquid or solid into a soft, semi-solid or solid mass.

Combustible

Capable of igniting and burning.

Combustion

A chemical change accompanied by the production of heat and light.

Concave

A curve that dips inward is considered concave. A concave lens is thinner in the middle than at the edge.

Convex

A curve that bulges outward is considered convex. A convex lens is thicker in the middle than at its edge.

Density

Thickness of consistency. The amount of something per unit of measure, i.e.: the weight as compared to size, the number of people as compared to a space, ect.

Disperse

To break up and scatter in various directions.

Diameter

The thickness or width of something.

Dissolve

To reduce to liquid form; to melt.

Electron

A subatomic particle that is negatively charged.

Exhale

To breathe out.

Extinguish

To cause to cease burning; to put an end to something.

Freezing Point

The temperature at which a liquid freezes and becomes a solid.

Frequency

The number of times a specified phenomenon occurs within a specified interval.

Friction

A rubbing of one object or surface against another.

Gas

The state of matter distinguished from solid and liquid states by very low density and relatively great expansion and contraction due to changes in pressure and temperature.

Glycerin

Glycerol; a syrupy, sweet, colorless liquid that is obtained from fats and oils. It is a byproduct of the manufacture of soaps and fatty acids.

Gravity

Sometimes called the "downward pull of the earth," gravity is the natural phenomenon of attraction between massive bodies and the action or process of moving under the influence of this attraction.

Hydrogen

A colorless, highly flammable gaseous element. It is the lightest of all gasses and is the most abundant gas in the universe.

Indicator

Any substance that changes color when it is added to an acid or a base.

Inertia

The tendency of a body at rest to remain at rest and a body in motion to remain in motion, unless disturbed by an external force.

Inflate

To expand; to fill up.

Inhale

To breathe in.

Insulation

Any material placed around an object that will not allow heat, electricity or sound to pass through.

Lens

A transparent material (usually glass) that has at least one curved surface.

Litmus

A blue powder that changes to red when with increasing acidity (acid) and to blue with increasing alkalinity (base).

Litmus paper

White paper infused with litmus and used as an acid-base indicator.

Lubricant

Usually an oily substance, such as grease, that reduces friction.

Magnification

The process of enlarging the size of something.

Matter

Anything that occupies space and can be perceived by one or more senses.

Membrane

A thin layer of tissue covering surfaces of an animal or plant.

Molecule

The smallest naturally occurring particle of a substance.

Non-Newtonian Fluid

Any substance that appears to have the properties of a solid and liquid at the same time; a suspension.

Nucleation

To bring together into a nucleus; the place where this happens is the nucleation site.

Nucleus

The central part around which other parts are grouped or collected.

Oxygen

A colorless, odorless and tasteless gaseous element essential for plant and animal respiration.

Particle

A very small piece or part of something.

Pigment

A substance used as coloring.

Pitch

Sound. Pitch is either considered high or low as determined by frequency.

Pressure

The application of continuous force by one body onto another; force applied over a surface.

Propel

To cause to move.

Propulsion

The process of driving or propelling something forward.

Puncture

To pierce with a pointed object.

Reaction

A reverse or opposing action. A response to a stimulus (an action) and the state resulting from such response.

Resistance

To work against; a force that opposes motion.

Sense Receptors

A group of cells receiving stimuli; the faculty of perceiving by means of the sense organs.

Sensory Adaptation

The process by which an organism adjusts to its environment.

Simultaneously

Happening at the same time.

Soluble

Capable of being dissolved; easily dissolved.

Solution

A mixture of two or more substances that form to create solids, liquids or gasses.

Static Electricity

An electrical discharge resulting from the accumulation of electric charge on an insulated body.

Surface Tension

Caused by unbalanced molecules at or near the surface of a liquid, surface tension causes the surface of a liquid to contract (pull together) and create a "skin," similar to a stretched elastic membrane, on the surface of the liquid.

Suspension

A mixture in which substances mix but do not dissolve.

Temperature

A measure of how hot or cold something is.

Time Warp

A distortion of time.

Vacuum

A state of being sealed off from external environmental influences; the absence of matter.

Vibration

A rapid, linear motion of a particle; a vibrating motion.

Viscosity

The degree to which a fluid resists flow when force is applied.

Viscous

Having high resistance to flow. A highly viscous liquid is one that flows slowly.

Index

t

v

w

water 11,14,19,23,25,27,28,29,31,32,33,34,36,37,39,44,45,46,48,49,51,53,54,55,57,58,59,62,63,64,65,66,67,68,69,70,71,72,73,74,75,77,81,84,86,87,90,91,93,94,96,97,103

   distilled water 29

watercolor see liquid watercolor, food coloring

waves 29,88,92

wax paper 15

whipping cream 15,24

white glue 26,47

whole milk 40

Windex® bottle 61

wine glass 14,67

Wintergreen Lifesavers® 41

wooden spoon 14,47,69

x

X-Acto® 57

y

yeast 15,97

yogurt container 14,85,92

z

Ziploc® Bag 15,26,47,56

Lisa Murphy is
the ooey gooey lady®!

Lisa Murphy, B.S., has been involved with early childhood education for over 20 years. She has taught and worked with children in various environments including Head Start programs, kindergarten, private schools, family childcare, park and rec centers, group homes and many child care centers.

Lisa is the founder and CEO of **Ooey Gooey, Inc.** As the *ooey gooey lady®*, Lisa presents over 150 workshops each year to audiences across the country on various topics related to early childhood education, specifically how to be more play-based in the classroom. She has been featured in various publications including *Child Care Business Exchange*, *Parents* and *Pre-K Today*. Lisa has authored four books and has created dozens of teacher training DVD's. A highly sought after keynoter for educational conferences, Lisa uses humor and real life anecdotes to reach and engage her audiences. Lisa's standing room only seminars have become nationally known for their information, humor, inspiration and energetic delivery. Frequently asked if she has ever been a stand up comic, Lisa practices what she preaches and continues to blend the laughter with the learning! Lisa has become known for her ability to link hands-on activities to educational standards and is dedicated to creating child-centered, play-based early childhood environments. Her commitment to reinforcing the importance of play in the lives of children is obvious in both her professional and personal life.

Lisa lives in Upstate New York with her husband Tom and their dog Otis. You can learn more about Lisa at **www.ooeygooey.com** and can follow her adventures on Facebook, YouTube and Twitter.

Notes !

Notes !

Notes !